The School at Crooked Creek

The
School at
Crooked
Creek

BY Laurie Lawlor

ILLUSTRATED BY
Ronald Himler

Holiday House / New York

Text copyright © 2004 by Laurie Lawlor
Illustrations copyright © 2004 by Ronald Himler
All Rights Reserved
Printed in the United States of America
www.holidayhouse.com
First Edition

1   3   5   7   9   10   8   6   4   2

Library of Congress Cataloging-in-Publication Data
Lawlor, Laurie.
The school at Crooked Creek / by Laurie Lawlor ;
illustrated by Ronald Himler.—1st ed.
        p.   cm.
Summary: Living on the 19th-century Indiana frontier with his
parents and irritable older sister Louise, six-year-old Beansie dreads
his first day of school, but his resilience surprises even his sister.
ISBN 0-8234-1812-X (hardcover)
[1. Frontier and pioneer life—Indiana—Fiction.   2. Schools—Fiction.
3. Brothers and sisters—Fiction.   4. Indiana—History—19th
century—Fiction.] I. Himler, Ronald, ill. II. Title.
PZ7.L4189Cp 2004
[Fic]—dc22
2003056759

For Ari

CONTENTS

✤

CHAPTER ONE	Winter's A-coming	1
CHAPTER TWO	Pap Makes Up His Mind	9
CHAPTER THREE	Louisa's Bumfuzzled	18
CHAPTER FOUR	Outrun, Outlick, Outholler	25
CHAPTER FIVE	A Sudden Case of Mulligrubs	32
CHAPTER SIX	A-going to School	40
CHAPTER SEVEN	Master Strike	49
CHAPTER EIGHT	No Half-pints Allowed	58
CHAPTER NINE	Bad-luck Signs	65
CHAPTER TEN	Backward and Forward	73

Crooked Creek

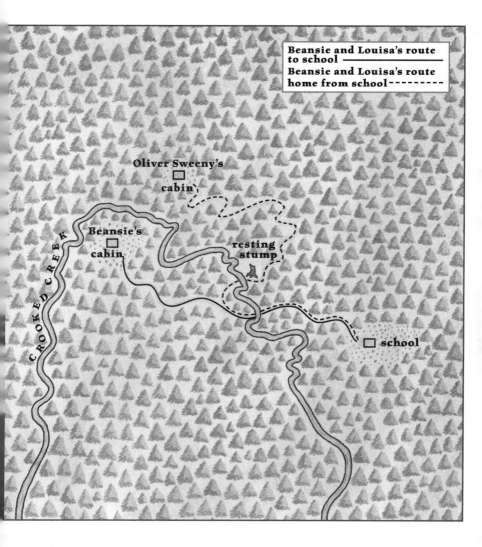

The School at Crooked Creek

CHAPTER ONE

❖

Winter's A-coming

When Beansie pulled off the blanket, he could see his breath. Quickly he snuggled back down into the warmth so that only his nose and mouth showed. "Winter's a-coming," he said in a confident voice nobody heard. His words floated up like haunts into the chill morning shadows of the loft where he slept. The ghostly shapes spooked him. Maybe they were some kind of sign. *Bide where you be.* He snuggled deeper, determined not to get out of bed until spring.

"Wake up, Beansie!" his older sister, Louisa, shouted up the loft ladder.

Beansie covered his face and made a snoring noise. He tried to ignore the tasty smell coming from downstairs—johnnycake baked on a clapboard tilted up before a good, warm fire.

CLUNK! Clunk-a-clunk! The floorboards jumped.

"No need to kick up a fuss," Beansie grumbled. He could never understand why every morning his nine-year-old sister took such pleasure in rapping the ceiling downstairs with the hard end of a broom.

"Your turn to fetch Bess," Louisa hollered. "Get moving, you no-count!"

Beansie rolled off his lumpy corncob pallet. He grabbed his shirt, clambered down the ladder, and lingered as long as he could near the fire in the big fireplace at one end of the log cabin. First he warmed his front and then his backside. Somewhere beyond the clearing he could hear the ringing sound of Pap's ax.

"If you want milk with breakfast," Ma said, "you better hurry up and find Bess." She bent before the fireplace's hard-packed clay hearth. Expertly, she took hold of one end of the clapboard, gave it a little shake to loosen the johnnycake, and flipped the corn bread up in the air to turn it over and catch it on the board. Then she set the johnnycake before the fire to finish baking.

Louisa paused while mixing cornmeal, salt, water, and butter for more johnnycake. She jutted a sticky thumb toward the door. "Get!" she growled. His sister had a bantam rooster's temper and red hair to match. Plenty of angry freckles disgraced her face, too. She wasn't one to tangle with in the morning.

Beansie stepped outside. Slowly he shifted from one bare foot to the other on a flat stone that felt colder than a dog's nose. He had to save his shoes for snowy days. Until it was shoe weather, he went barefoot and tried to keep from stepping on prickers, brambles, and acorns.

A fine mist rolled across the stumpy clearing that surrounded the one-room, eighteen-by-twenty-foot cabin. No other house could be seen beyond the trees. Beansie took a deep breath. There was a bigness and a certain moldy smell to the forest—a mighty sweet and satisfying aroma of damp wood and rotting leaves.

Pap said that woods stretched for miles in all

directions in this part of central Indiana. "Finest building timber you ever saw. One day Indianapolis will grow to be a big town," Pap liked to say of the nearest settlement, which was nearly a day's journey on foot there and back.

Trips to town to buy gunpowder or salt or to have the plow sharpened at the blacksmith's were rare. The family grew, hunted, gathered, or made most everything they needed. Beansie had never traveled far beyond his family's clearing. Indianapolis seemed impossibly distant.

A cold wind rustled through the leaves. Beansie crossed his arms in front of his skinny body and held his elbows tight for warmth.

Carefully he listened for the deep, grave sound of the cow's bell in the distance. Somewhere beyond the closest ring of trees, Bess was probably munching whatever scraggly greens grew on the forest floor. If the bell hanging around her neck made an irregular sound, Beansie knew it meant Bess was eating and mostly staying in one place. But if the bell made a steady *dong-dong-dong* sound, she was gallivanting through the woods. The annoying animal traipsed away

whenever she had the chance—just to make his life miserable.

"Beansie!" Ma called from the cabin. "Get up on your get-alongs and find that cow!"

"Yes, ma'am." He grabbed his lucky stick that was leaning against the cabin wall and set off into the woods. The trees stood so close together that little sunlight ever reached the forest floor. A dull green twilight hung over everything. Sometimes hours after sunrise, the woods still dripped with dew. Even at noon on a bright day, the forest was cool and dark. Today the forest seemed gloomier than ever. Beansie hated searching for Bess when the woods were especially dark and scawmy. Anything could be hiding in the mist.

A creature skittered past and kicked up a ruckus in the leaves. Beansie froze. Only a squirrel. He kept walking, slower now—trying to keep his heart from beating so loud. Branches broke. Beansie whirled. Only a sleepy raccoon stumbling over a fallen tree. Beansie aimed his stick. As soon as he was big enough to tote a gun, Pap said he'd teach him to shoot. Might be a long time, seeing how long it was taking six-year-old Beansie to grow. He kicked a pile of bright leaves. What if he never got any bigger? What if he never learned to shoot?

"Bess!" Beansie shouted, then listened for the *dong-dong-dong*. Ordinarily he found her right away just by following the sound. Where could she be? He turned and tried to memorize the way he'd come. It was easy enough to be turned around and around where the trees grew thick.

"Bess?" Beansie called. His stomach growled. He wanted to turn around and go home, where it was warm and his breakfast was waiting.

He heard claws scratch bark. Something thrashed in the underbrush. Beansie gulped. He remembered Pap's words: "Panther's been bothering the chickens again." A panther's big yellow eyes might be watching him right now, staring down from the high treetops. Licking its lips, sharp teeth shining.

Beansie felt too scared to breathe, too scared to run. Suddenly he couldn't remember how he'd come. Which direction was home? He stood perfectly still. Was that the sound of a cowbell or the *chink-a-chink* of a chickadee?

A sapling snapped. Something heavy pushed past tangled branches. *Moooo!* The familiar lowing brought Beansie back to his senses. "Bess!" he cried. The bony old cow shook her head at him as if she thought he was a sorry sight. Woods didn't bother her. The cow knew how to go home when she was ready.

Beansie unwound the vine that had caught around her neck and silenced her bell clapper. "Come on, Bess," he said, glad to have somebody to talk to on the walk back.

CHAPTER TWO

❖

Pap Makes Up His Mind

When Beansie spied his sister waiting in the clearing, he called, "Found Bess!" Then he strutted with his walking stick past the family's jabbering trio of chickens.

"What took you so long? That cow was probably in plain view the whole time," Louisa said. She scattered a handful of precious corn for the hungry chickens.

Beansie made a face at his sister and kept strutting. He didn't want Louisa to know how scared he had been back there in the woods.

"Where do you think you're going? You can help."

Beansie hooked his thumb in his linen shirt,

the way he'd seen Pap do. He stood as tall as he could. "Milking's a girl's job."

"Now ain't you awful high and mighty this morning," Louisa said, then added with a sly smile, "Too bad no Injun tried scalping you."

"Injun?" Beansie gulped.

Louisa smiled. "Ask Pap." Then she led Bess away for milking.

Beansie leaned his walking stick against the cabin. He listened. Where was Pap? There was no sound of his father chopping beyond the clearing.

Cutting away two acres of trees and brush had taken Pap more than a year of everlasting work. Trees eighteen inches in diameter and under were felled with an ax and burned. Stouter trees were left standing to save time. The smell of smoke lingered everywhere as Pa plowed the ground around the blackened stumps. He was the only one strong enough to manage the ox when the plow bucked and cut through popping roots.

Soon as the elm tree leaves were the size of a squirrel's ear in spring, the whole family had planted corn. Now the spindly green plants were bent with heavy ears.

"Get!" Beansie shouted at a big blackbird that lighted on a precious cornstalk. Beansie waved his arms. The bird flapped its shimmering wings and flew away.

Beansie cocked his head to one side. His father's voice rumbled from inside the one-room cabin. Beansie slunk through the door. He found Pap sitting on a bench at the rough-hewn table. Pap was nursing his sore elbow with a poultice made from jimsonweed. Some days he could hardly swing an ax, the swelling was so bad.

"Buckle down, boy," Pap said when he saw Beansie. Pap had the same wiry dark hair and quick dark eyes as Beansie. "Your ma shouldn't have to wait on you when there's work to be done."

"Yes, sir," Beansie said. He cleared his throat. Maybe this wasn't a good time to ask questions about skulking Indians.

"Sit, Beansie," Ma said. She plunked roughly carved wooden bowls filled with cornmeal mush onto the table. Louisa came inside and carefully lowered a bucket of milk onto the splintery cabin floor made of short oak boards. Ma ladled fresh milk into each trencher. Nobody spoke as they ate.

Pap scraped his trencher clean. He looked at Beansie and Louisa. "Pretty soon it will be time for you to start school. Come December a new schoolmaster's going to begin at the schoolhouse. I aim to send you both a whole term—December, January, and February."

Beansie slumped forward and rested his chin on the table. He should have stayed in bed. He knew it. This news was bad. Very bad.

Louisa's face flushed with delight. "When do we start?" She'd been to school in Virginia in 1825, the year before the family came to Indiana. She liked nothing better than to tell Beansie about her days reading and writing, sitting indoors all day long. Sometimes they sang songs, she said. Sometimes they played spelling games.

School sounded like some kind of torture to Beansie. He couldn't stand the idea of being trapped in a dark, crowded cabin, singing and playing stupid games when there was plenty to do outdoors. Besides, what use was there in learning how to spell? And there didn't seem much point in reading, either, as far as he could tell. Ma couldn't read. Pap knew how, but he was too busy to teach them.

"When?" Louisa demanded again.

"Soon enough," Ma said. Her voice sounded uncertain. That gave Beansie hope. Maybe he could change Ma's mind.

"How long is 'soon enough'?" Louisa asked.

"Come snow time," Pap said and laughed. "Don't worry. We'll keep track so you won't miss the first day of school."

"Is it far?" Beansie said in a small voice. He shrank down so that his eyes barely peeked over the edge of the table. Then he shot his mother a woesome glance.

Ma pursed her lips. "Bartholomew's no bigger than a cake of soap after a week's wash," she said to Pap, as if Beansie weren't there. For once she used Beansie's real name, which sounded far too large for a boy his size.

"Do I have to go, Pap?" Beansie screwed up his face so that he looked like he was about to whimper. "The woods are big and dark."

Pap didn't answer.

"How are his short legs going to carry him that long, long way?" Má asked in a worried voice.

"Don't expect me to tote you on my back," Louisa whispered to Beansie. "I've got to save my strength for ciphering and learning to read."

Ma was so busy discussing Beansie's small size that she and Pap didn't hear a word Louisa said. "...short growth for sure. Don't you recollect back in Virginia, when Beansie was three years old, how you bore the hole in that tree to his exact height? Then we stuffed the hole with a lock of his hair, hoping as the tree grew, so would he. You remember, don't you?"

Pap nodded. He drummed the table with his calloused fingers.

"And there's always a chance they'll get lost. It's more than a mile between our place and the school," Ma continued. "Poor Beansie! He'll die of fright."

The back of Beansie's neck prickled. He had heard the story of the hole-in-the-tree cure a hundred times, but he'd never heard that somebody could die of fright. *Could that happen to me?* Right away he thought of the most fearsome thing he knew. "Pap, what about Injuns creeping about? What if we get scalped going to school?"

Pap hooted. "Ain't no skulking Injuns in the woods anymore. Who told you such nonsense?"

Beansie shot his sister a nasty look. Louisa just smiled. She seemed delighted to have fooled him with such a whopping lie.

Pap rubbed his elbow. "Sending Beansie and Louisa's a real sacrifice. I've got more work to do than I can shake a stick at."

Beansie brightened. "I can stay home and help you, Pap."

Pap shook his head. "Book-learning's important. It's only a short while that you'll be in school. A couple months. There's things you got to learn, Beansie."

Beansie frowned. "Yes, sir." He couldn't think of one thing he wanted to learn. Being trapped in school for a couple months sounded as pleasant as being a catfish choked to death on a sandbank.

The worst of it, Beansie knew, was that he'd have to risk his life every day, journeying through unfamiliar, dark woods—past panthers and who knew what. School sounded as far away as Indianapolis. He'd rather stay home and gather brush or hoe corn or scare off big blackbirds. Never again would he complain about fetching Bess if Pap would let him skip school. He took a deep breath. "Pap?" he asked, ready to tell his father how he'd do anything without complaining or shirking from now on. "I—"

Boom! His father thumped the table with his fist, the way he did when he brooked no argument. "I've made up my mind. Louisa and Beansie are both a-going to school." Pap stood up and reached for the ax. "Come on, Beansie. We got work to do."

CHAPTER THREE

❖

Louisa's Bumfuzzled

Days passed. The woods seemed impatient with changing color, changing sounds. Sumac exploded in deep red. Wild grapes deepened to dark purple. Swarms of geese honked overhead. Big fish thrashed upriver.

In bright sunlight the sugar maples glinted with what looked like dangling red rags. When the wind howled, poplars and sycamores, hickories and chestnuts unleashed showers of diving, twisting yellow leaves. Sometimes the leaves sailed straight up, sometimes down, sometimes sideways. Beansie held out his arms and closed his eyes tight. Leaves swirled around him and hissed, *"Bean-seee! Bean-seee!"*

Fresh-fallen leaves drifted so deep in places that he had to wade through them waist-deep. Leaves scudded and skittered around him as he paddled his arms and pretended to swim. *Whoosh whoosh-a-whoosh!* The tangy smell reminded Beansie of the deer hides Pap worked into leather.

There was always something for Beansie to do. Every day he gathered kindling and wood chips for the fireplace. He slopped the cow and fed the chickens. He yanked the butter churn handle up and down till the butter was too stiff to budge. When it was about to rain, he set out wooden buckets to collect water. And when washday came, he helped Ma hang wet clothes on the bushes to dry. At night he brought the clothes inside.

As soon as he finished his chores, he was free to climb trees or do as he wished. One particular morning he decided to shimmy up an oak he'd been eying for some time. Gnarly-limbed and coarse-furrowed, the tree had an inviting size to it. Not too big. Not too little.

Once he climbed up to the first big branch, he looked up and saw just where to reach next. He always made sure the branch was strong enough to hold him before he put his full weight on it—skinny as he was. Up and up and up he went until the branches grew too spindly to bear him.

He seated himself on a safe, high place and dangled his feet. It was so peaceful up in the oak. Nobody could see him hidden among the leaves that had turned from red to bronze to brown. Nobody could bother him. Not even Louisa.

Wind creaked the branches. The leaves danced and chattered. But Beansie wasn't scared. He felt big. He felt powerful. If he wanted to, maybe he could fly. He'd stretch out his arms and glide like a leaf. He'd swoop around and make daring loops in the air. And then wouldn't Louisa be surprised?

Beansie watched the clouds in a blue patch of sky overhead. He felt so pleased with himself he began to sing softly the words Ma had taught him:

"It's step her to your weev'ly wheat,
It's step her to your barley,

20

It's *step her to your weev'ly wheat*
To bake a cake for Charley."

High up in the branches was a private, secret place nobody knew about except him. He could do whatever he wanted. He spit as far as he could. He chucked acorns at neighboring trees. Suddenly he heard a familiar voice. He froze and stared down between his dangling feet. Far, far below was Louisa, who mumbled words to no one in particular—words Beansie couldn't hear.

His sister seemed unaware that Beansie was spying on her as she bent over and brushed something into a noggin. Did Ma know Louisa had taken one of the precious wooden mugs from the cabin? Beansie strained to see what she might be picking. Weren't any papaws down there, far as he could remember. No hickory nuts, either. The only decent hackberry tree nearby had already been stripped of fruit.

What was she gathering so carefully? Beansie craned his neck. For a second he glimpsed the inside of the noggin.

Nothing. She was gathering nothing.

Beansie scowled. What was wrong with Louisa? Talking to herself and scooping up invisible bits. Beansie watched, certain that his sister was bumfuzzled. *Wait until I tell Ma. Louisa's gone stark crazy.*

Beansie scooted over for a better look. When he did, the tree pelted down a half-dozen acorns. Louisa looked up, startled, and saw her brother peering down at her. "What you think you're doing?" she said, mad as a wet hen.

"What you think *you're* doing?" Beansie echoed. He smiled. He hadn't felt so proud of himself in a very long time. For once he had given his sister her comeuppance. "What you got there?"

Louisa made a sour face. She hid the noggin behind her back. "Nothing."

"Then why you hiding it?"

She scowled. "Pap's looking for you. Better climb down lickety-split."

He knew change-the-subject was Louisa's favorite trick. "You're bumfuzzled, Louisa."

"Am not."

"Why you collecting nothing in that noggin?

22

Ma said nobody's supposed to take the good mugs from the cabin."

"Can do as I please." She glared at him. Her face turned bright red. "Better not tell."

Beansie licked his lips. *Look how I aggrafret her!* "Can do as I please," he taunted.

Louisa took a deep breath, puffed her cheeks out like a bullfrog, and let the air out all at once. She put her fists on her waist. "Come down and swear you won't tell nobody, and I'll do half your chores for you for a week."

"A week?" This seemed impossibly long to Beansie.

"All right, two weeks."

Beansie smiled.

"Now climb down and swear you won't tell."

CHAPTER FOUR

❖

Outrun, Outlick, Outholler

Beansie grabbed hold of a nearby branch. Carefully he swung his feet around and tried to feel for the next lowest place to stand.

"Hurry up!" Louisa shouted.

Beansie glanced down. The sight of his sister—so furious, so tiny—on the ground far, far below suddenly made him queasy.

"Don't got all day."

Beansie didn't say anything. He did not like anyone watching him when he climbed down—especially someone as critical as Louisa. Going down was always much more difficult than going up. For one thing, he couldn't see where his next foothold might be. If he looked down, the uncertain movement of branches and leaves below made him feel as nervous as a cat in a room full of rocking chairs.

"Come on, slowpoke."

"I'm hurrying," Beansie muttered. He tried to move more quickly. He grabbed a branch. The branch bent. He snagged another, just in the nick of time.

Louisa laughed. "Ain't much of a squirrel, are you?"

Sweat poured down Beansie's arms. He wanted his sister to go away and stop watching so he could concentrate. Slowly but surely he made his way down the tree. At last he stood on solid ground. He leaned forward, hands on his knees, breathing heavily—nearly petered out.

"Got a bellyache?" Louisa asked.

He shook his head. He took a gulp of air and stood up. His shoulders slumped forward. Whatever power and peacefulness he had experienced high in the oak were gone. He felt puny and anxious again. Warily he looked at his sister. "You say you'll do half my chores?"

"For two weeks, long as you swear you won't tell nobody," Louisa said.

"What I seen you collect?" Beansie peered into the noggin, which seemed to have a few drops of clear liquid in it. "Don't look like much. What is it?"

Louisa kept her mouth shut tight.

After all Beansie had been through climbing down, he felt he had the right to know. "Better say or I'll tell Ma you took her good noggin outside in the damp."

Louisa's eyes narrowed. She clenched her teeth. "Cobweb dew."

"What?"

"You heard me."

Beansie rubbed the back of his head. He glanced about the bushes and saw dangling webs of spiders glistening with jewel-like beads of dew. "What you need cobweb dew for?"

Louisa coughed. "That's for me to know and you to find out."

Beansie crossed his arms in front of himself. "Better say or I tell Ma."

Louisa flushed a brighter shade of red. "Freckles," she mumbled.

He looked at her with astonishment. *Bumfuzzled for sure.* Louisa's face was so full of freckles, there scarcely seemed room for more. "Where you going to put the extras?"

"I don't want *more* freckles," she replied in a haughty manner. "Cobweb dew gets rid of what I got."

"Oh," Beansie replied, still confused. "What do you do? Rub it on your face?"

She nodded, then looked away. She didn't say anything for several moments.

"That works?"

She nodded.

He wondered. Maybe there might be some kind of cure to make him grow. Some kind of special tonic. "What makes you so sure?"

"Everybody knows cobweb dew works. Same as sassafras tea cures a crick in your back or rubbing a raw potato takes away a wart."

Beansie looked at his sister suspiciously. She had told him a whopper before about the scalping Indian. How could he be sure she wasn't lying to him again? "How come you're in such an all-fired hurry to get rid of your freckles?"

Louisa sighed. "Don't have much time before school starts."

Beansie frowned. He didn't want to think about school. Secretly he had been hoping everyone would forget about the idea. "What's wrong with freckles at school?" he asked nervously.

Louisa bit her lip. She didn't speak.

Beansie waited. He dug his dirty toe into the ground. He waited. Still she didn't say anything. He snuck a glimpse of Louisa's sad face. Maybe she wasn't as nasty as he thought. "Well," he said in a slow, encouraging voice, "I don't think you look so bad."

"What do *you* know?" she demanded. "Oliver Sweeny says I got a face as freckled as a turkey egg."

A turkey egg. Beansie felt so surprised he couldn't speak.

"You've never been to school." Louisa's eyes flashed with anger. "You don't know anything."

Beansie edged away from his sister as if she were as unpredictable and dangerous as fire. He would never understand Louisa. Never.

Oliver Sweeny and his family lived way on the other side of Crooked Creek. They hardly ever saw Oliver. They hardly ever saw anybody. Last time Oliver strolled through their clearing—a couple of weeks ago—he had knocked Louisa into a mud puddle. Oliver claimed he could outrun, outlick, outholler anybody. And Beansie believed him. Anybody who dared call Louisa a turkey egg and shove her into the mud had to be just about the bravest boy Beansie knew.

"Stop standing there with your mouth open like you're trapping flies," Louisa snapped. "Come on. Pap's waiting. He wants you to help him with some special chore." She held the noggin carefully and marched away toward the clearing. She moved so fast that Beansie could barely keep up.

CHAPTER FIVE

❖

A Sudden Case
of Mulligrubs

Beansie hurried inside the cabin. He didn't have a chance to ask about the special chore before Pap was out the door. Beansie kept close to Pap's heels and tried as best he could to match his father's long strides with his puny half steps. He didn't want Pap to think he was too short in the britches and couldn't keep up. When they came to the edge of the clearing, Pap plunged into the undergrowth. He toted the ax with special care so it didn't nick or drop. "Come on," Pap called. "You watch where we go and help tote branches out of the way."

Beansie struggled with all his might to do what Pap said, but he kept falling farther and farther behind. Pap stopped every so often and chopped away branches and brush. Then he made a mark

on the nearest tree trunk, a quick, low gash that looked to Beansie like a sad eye. What did it mean? Why was Pap clearing a trail in this direction?

When they came to Crooked Creek, Pap stopped, brushed away the fallen leaves, and dipped his strong hands into the shallow current. Red-faced, Beansie kneeled beside him and did the same. The water felt cool and refreshing. The creek's friendly noise and the dancing sunlight made Beansie think about fishing. He wished they could just sit here and dangle a line. But Pap seemed in too much of a hurry.

"Where we making trail to, Pap?" Beansie asked. Such work seemed important and grown-up. He sat on the muddy bank and put one foot into the water, then the other, the same way he'd seen Pap do.

"To the schoolhouse." Pap stood up and wiped his mouth with the back of his hand.

Beansie slumped forward. He felt trapped. "Is it 'soon enough' already?"

Pap nodded. "Few more weeks. Come on. We don't have much daylight."

Miserable, Beansie staggered to his feet. He

felt overwhelmed by a sudden case of mulligrubs. He was too discouraged to clear trail anymore. Reluctantly he rubbed one wet foot then the other against the back of each leg of his britches. He trudged behind Pap as he hacked away underbrush. Beansie dragged chopped branches to the sides of the trail that he was convinced would take him to his doom.

As Pap worked he sang:

"Coon he has a ringsey tail,
Possum's tail is baar,
Rabbit hain't no tail at all
But a leetle brush o' haar."

Beansie worked slower and slower.

"How come you ain't singing?" Pap asked.

Beansie shrugged. "Don't feel like rolling a song, I guess." He dropped a big branch. "You go to school, Pap?"

"Not unless you call two weeks in school book-learning. My pa made me quit so I could plow. I learned to read from my mother." He swung the ax and made another mark.

"Pap, what's it like in school?"

"Thought Louisa told you."

"She only said certain things," Beansie said in a slow, careful voice. He didn't mention freckles. He didn't mention turkey eggs. After all, he didn't want Pap to laugh at him again about something Louisa had told him. Beansie wasn't sure if he could trust his sister as far as he could throw a bull by the tail.

Pap paused. "There's a whole passel of young 'uns at school. All different ages. Mostly older than you, I suspect."

Beansie had never thought about the other children at school. He didn't have any friends. He never considered he needed any. Beansie never felt lonely. The clearing near the cabin was inhabited by all manner of interesting creatures. Snakes curled in warm, sunny places. Squirrels came to visit. Daddy longlegs wobbled through the long grass. If he was lucky, he'd be right on the spot when young spiders ballooned and sailed away.

The last time the preacher came through was the last time Beansie was surrounded by a half-dozen children his own age. He had been too shy to stray from Ma. He kept a careful distance and watched the children, who seemed as savage as wild boars as they chased each other with sharp sticks outside the cabin during prayer services. They set his secret fort on fire. If everyone at school was as wolfish as those children, he didn't want to go. He was absolutely certain.

"Beansie, haul that pile of brush," Pap called. He had moved far ahead while Beansie was busy worrying.

"Yes, sir." Beansie sighed. He wished he were Pap, all grown-up and through with school. Pap knew everything—how to tell the weather from what the sunset and the sky said. He could predict what would happen when there was a moist south wind or a dry one out of the east. Why couldn't Beansie learn from Pap what was important? He didn't need to go to school.

Beansie leaned over and watched a brown and black caterpillar slink across the new path. He coaxed the tickly caterpillar to climb along his finger. "Hello, woolly bear," Beansie said. "You don't have to go to school neither, do you?" Carefully he placed the caterpillar back on a leaf. When he looked up, Pap was so far ahead that Beansie could no longer see him. He could only hear the sound of the ax.

Beansie glanced between the trees and spied a deer path. The trails made by deer herds looked like a person made them, Pap once told Beansie. "Sometimes these trails coax you to come on," Pap said. "They seem to say, 'We'll take you out of the woods—maybe to a clearing.' Don't believe them. You follow a deer path, you'll turn and twist and circle and end up in the middle of a swamp."

Beansie shivered. When the endless forest overwhelmed and confused a person so badly they panicked and wandered lost and never came home, that was called "woods fever." Pap told him woods fever came upon him once. But he managed to calm himself by sitting on a stump and saying the name of every hunting dog he had as a boy. When he finished he stood up and remembered which way was which. That was how he got home.

The forest seemed darker. Between the tops of the bare trees, Beansie saw bruised gray clouds gathering. Wind shoved and tangled the tops of the bare trees so they made a hollow O-sound. The air felt sharp and cold and smelled of snow—a damp, gray odor that stung the inside of his nose. Beansie wrapped his shirt close about himself. He hoped he never had woods fever. As fast as he could, he hurried to catch up with Pap.

CHAPTER SIX

❖

A-going to School

One night a few weeks later, the first snow of the season fell. When Beansie woke up, his blanket was heaped with white that had drifted indoors through the gaps between the wooden clapboards that covered the cabin roof. He shook off the snow and threw back the blanket. Louisa was finished helping with half his chores. She had held up her end of the bargain for two weeks. Now it was his turn to gather all the kindling Ma needed for the fire.

He was halfway down the ladder from the loft when he remembered. *Today's the first day of school.*

He would have slunk back up to hide in the freezing loft if his sister hadn't been watching him. She sat on a three-legged stool beside the fire and pressed something to her face.

"You ailing with a toothache?" Beansie asked and crept closer. He knew how frightful a throbbing tooth felt.

Louisa shook her head. She pressed a cloth to another part of her face.

"Chill and fever maybe?"

Louisa turned and looked at him with distaste. "Go away and leave me be."

Beansie trudged to the door. No use trying to be understanding to somebody as nasty as Louisa. Only get his head bit off.

Wearily Beansie pulled on the stiff shoes Pap had made from oxhide. As soon as he opened the door, he could see that everything had changed. The trees and stumps, bushes and garden glistened with a thin layer of white. There wasn't enough snow to make a good-sized snowball, but the clearing looked magical nonetheless.

Across the clearing Ma trudged toward him with her heavy shawl wrapped around her shoulders. A long gray strand of hair whipped every which way in the wind. She carried a heavy pail of milk. "Where's your sister?"

"Inside," Beansie replied. "She sick?"

Ma sighed. "Sick with worry maybe. That's all."

Beansie felt confused. Could someone get sick from worry? Was that like dying from fright?

Ma lowered the pail to the ground. She took Beansie's troubled face between her rough hands and gently tilted his head back, as if to get a better look at him. Her dark eyes shone like black water. He felt embarrassed. He wasn't used to shows of affection from his mother.

Ma made a whispery little arc on his cheek with her thumb. "Can't imagine why a few freckles could cause so much fret." She let go of Beansie, then wrapped her shawl tighter around her thin shoulders. "Wouldn't keep *me* from school, you can be right sure about that."

"Louisa's not going to school?" Relief washed over Beansie. If she stayed home, certainly so could he.

Ma shook her head. "She's a-going. She's just afraid the other children will make fun of her."

"For freckles?" Beansie asked. School was sounding worse and worse by the moment.

"No amount of cobweb dew'll change anything. I told her. She won't listen. But she's a-going to school. And that's that." Ma picked up the pail and started for the door. "Get me some good kindling, Beansie. None of the green stuff."

"Yes, ma'am," Beansie replied, still feeling disappointed. There seemed no escape. If Louisa could not convince Ma to let her stay home from school, how could he?

When they all sat down for breakfast, Pap told Louisa and Beansie to stop looking like the hind wheels of bad luck. Beansie tried to make a brave face. Louisa kept pouting. "Now you know the way, don't you, Beansie?" Pap demanded.

Beansie nodded halfheartedly.

"It's just a dusting of snow out there. It'll burn off in an hour or two," Pap said. "You can see those blaze marks I made along the trail clear as day."

"If you feel tired, Beansie, rest awhile on a log," Ma said.

"Keep your eyes peeled for Oliver Sweeny and follow him," Pap said. "He's starting school, too, and he's sure to pass this way."

"Oh, Pap!" Louisa cried in alarm. "Oliver is so ornery that the dogs won't bark at him. He chucks rocks and pulls my hair." She rubbed her freckly cheek hard, then stared in disappointment at her hand.

Pap shot Louisa a stern glance. It was clear he would tolerate no more of her complaints. "Oliver knows these woods backward and forward. Just keep your distance and follow which way he goes."

Beansie's stomach fluttered. He wasn't sure he wanted to follow a fellow who could outrun, outlick, outholler anybody—even his sister.

When the breakfast dishes were washed, Beansie and Louisa set off down the path through the big woods to school. Pap waved. Ma dabbed her eyes with her apron.

Beansie swung his dinner bucket so hard that his chunk of hoecake made a good, loud clunk. He liked that noise. Carrying his very own corn bread in his very own dinner bucket made him feel grown-up. His shoes made squeaking noises in the snow. Sure enough, it wasn't a hardship to follow Pap's blaze marks.

As he followed his sister, he glanced up, between the trees. Gray clouds galloped overhead. Bare branches sang in the wind, "*Bean-seee! Bean-seee!*" What were the trees trying to tell him?

Louisa paused and looked down the trail, the way they had come. *Crunch-crunch-crunch.* "Somebody's following us," she said in a low voice.

Sure enough, a boy wearing a brand-spang-new green scarf trudged toward them, head bent, shoulders forward. "Oliver Sweeny!" she said in a fearful voice. She grabbed Beansie's hand. "Whatever you do, don't aggrafret him."

Beansie and Louisa flew up the hill, around the trees, down the hill, through the brush, and over Crooked Creek. They ran so fast that Beansie forgot his legs might be too small to carry him.

As soon as they arrived at the clearing near the schoolhouse, Louisa dropped her brother's hand. Beansie was plumb out of breath. He studied the herd of children lingering in the beatdown ground near the log schoolhouse. A few

made marks in the snow with their heels. Most hooted and hollered or rassled. They kicked up a ruckus, butting each other like deer or jumping over each other like frogs.

Beansie had never seen so many wild, noisy children in one place before in his life. He bit his lip. He didn't feel very grown-up anymore.

"Don't bother me," Louisa warned Beansie. "And don't cry or cause trouble."

Before Beansie could say a word, he found himself abandoned at the edge of the clearing. He watched his sister wander carefully toward the edge of the group. None of the children acted cruel and shouted, "Freckles!" As far as Beansie could tell, they did not seem to notice Louisa at all.

"Come to books!" a large man shouted. He stood in the doorway and rang a bell. *Dong-dong-dong!* The herd stampeded toward the door and disappeared inside the leaning, squat log building that sat whopperjawed beside a scraggly pine. When everyone was inside, the man glanced around the clearing. He frowned when he noticed Beansie shivering in the shadows. "Hurry up, boy!"

At that moment Beansie almost darted into the brush and scurried toward home. But the man's fiery stare kept him frozen to the spot. "You coming?" the man bellowed. "Don't make me give you a dose of hickory tea!"

Beansie gulped. He didn't know what hickory tea was, but he was sure it wasn't good. Fast as Beansie could pick 'em up and lay 'em down, he hurried to the schoolhouse door.

CHAPTER SEVEN

❖

Master Strike

The first thing Beansie noticed inside the crooked schoolhouse was the terrifying forest of heads and arms and legs and feet. The rowdy students squirmed and wiggled in row upon row of crude benches. The benches, made from halves of peeled logs, sat round side up on wooden legs. Shoulder to shoulder, the biggest boys had planted themselves in the row closest to the door. Their backs towered like a grove of giant poplars. A few twisted in their seats and shot menacing glances at Beansie.

I don't have any freckles. Why do they look at me so mean? Beansie scurried away. Where should he go? He searched frantically around the stuffy room that smelled of sweat and unwashed clothing. There seemed to be no empty space left.

For a moment he spotted his sister's bright red hair and nearly cried out her name. Then he remembered her warning: *Don't bother me.*

"Sit down!" the big man at the front of the room barked. Beansie slunk to a bench right in front. The bench was already crowded with two girls with matching runny noses and a slouching fat boy.

With great difficulty, Beansie climbed onto the slippery round top of the bench. Just when he thought he had a good grip and was nearly astride the wooden beast, he lost his balance and tumbled backward. *Crash!* He landed in a heap on the hard-packed dirt floor.

The room exploded with earsplitting laughter.

The big man with the bell slammed a piece of wood against a table at the front of the room. The schoolroom became silent. Shamefaced, Beansie crawled back onto the slick bench and held on as tightly as if his life depended on it.

"My name is Master Strike," the big man said. His booming voice startled Beansie so much that he nearly fell off the bench again. "I am your schoolmaster. Here are my rules. . . ."

Beansie rubbed his bruised back and studied Master Strike's face. His sleepy eyes looked like two burned holes in a blanket. When he talked, the mole on his chin jumped. Beansie watched, fascinated. And when he grew tired of watching Master Strike's mole, he studied the classroom's only window.

The window was a narrow space to Beansie's left that ran along one side of the room. It looked like a log had been removed. The window had wooden strips pinned up and down across the opening. Greased paper was fastened between the strips—just like the one window in Beansie's family's cabin. Beneath the classroom's dimly lit opening was a long table cluttered with interesting objects: feathers and strips of brown paper. To Beansie's right was a fireplace in which a feeble fire smoldered.

". . . First lesson—'rithmetic," Master Strike boomed. "Get your Pike's 'rithmetic."

There was a mad scramble as the students around Beansie reached under their benches for a book, a slate, and a slate pencil. Beansie didn't have a book or a slate or a pencil, so he looked over at the slate held by the pudgy boy sitting next to him. Beansie couldn't make out what any of the scrawl on the slate meant. He started to sweat.

"Know how to count?" Master Strike asked, scanning the first row. One of the girls was so frightened, she burst into tears. "Here, copy this." Master Strike pointed to a row of strange shapes on his own slate. Then he hurried on to the next row.

Luckily for Beansie, the boy sitting next to him seemed to know what to do. He pressed the pencil to the slate and drew sleeping snakes, curled snakes, curved snakes. Beansie watched in amazement. "What's that?" Beansie whispered. "Copperheads?"

"Numbers," the boy replied, as if Beansie were as dull as a fence post. "Know what wakes up snakes first thing in the spring?"

Beansie shook his head. He was too fascinated by the venomous shapes to speak.

"Thunder." The pudgy boy looked victorious. He made a whooshing sound through his O-shaped mouth. His breath smelled like dead skunk.

Beansie was going to ask him what he ate for breakfast, when Master Strike started hollering again. "Get your writin' lesson."

The biggest students elbowed their way to the table at the side of the room. A few of the quieter ones picked up the feathers and carefully dipped them into bottles, then scratched the tips on paper. *Scritch-scritch-a-scritch.* The squeaky sounds they made reminded Beansie of mice in a haystack. "What are they doing?" Beansie asked Skunk Breath.

"Practicing handwriting with quill pens, ink, and foolscap paper." He rolled his eyes. "Only the old scholars get to. We got to use slates." He wiped his nose with the back of his dirty hand. Then he wiped off the slate board. "You know your A–B–C?"

Beansie shook his head. He was feeling more and more stupid by the moment.

"I can write my name," Skunk Breath said. "See?"

Beansie studied the scribble. "What's it say?"

"L–U–K–E," Skunk Breath replied in a biggety voice that made him sound all swelled up like a pizzened pup.

"Oh," said Beansie. He sighed and stared at the dim light coming through the window. Would he ever get out of this place? His legs were falling asleep. He was afraid to move his feet, which were hanging in midair, because he knew he'd fall off the bench for sure. The only way he could rest was to hunker down with his elbows on his knees and carefully slide back a little.

"I'll wear you out if you don't behave!" Master Strike threatened the boys cutting a caper in the back of the room. "Now pay attention: 'A' is for *apple*." Master Strike made some marks on a slate. The marks didn't look one bit like an apple. All Beansie could think of was how much he wanted to escape and climb the apple tree back home. "'B' is for *bear*."

Skunk Breath made a shape that looked like a tipped-over mushroom. It didn't make one bit of sense to Beansie. Where was the bear?

Next came the spelling lesson. Everyone shouted words and letters at once. The girl on the bench behind Beansie bellowed so powerfully that he thought everyone else might as well just lay their books down.

Skunk Breath jutted a thumb in the noisy girl's direction. "Talks to hear her brains rattle."

When Master Strike wasn't looking, Beansie put his hands over his ears.

"Noon recess!" Master Strike shouted.

Grateful, Beansie slid off the bench. There seemed to be scarcely any air left in the room. His legs felt like rubber. He knew better than to get in the way of the stampede and waited for the others to grab their coats and dinner buckets, and push their way outside. Beansie was so tired as he shuffled toward the door that it seemed as if one foot was saying to the other, "You let me pass you this time and I'll let you pass me next time."

A large hand plunked on the top of Beansie's head and stayed there like a heavy hat. Startled, Beansie stood perfectly still.

"How old are you?" a voice boomed from behind.

"Six, sir," Beansie squawked. The big hand could belong to only one person. His teacher.

"You're so small," Master Strike said in a more kindly tone, "I bet you have to stand in the same place twice to make a shadow."

"Yes, sir," Beansie said. He just wanted to escape. *Let me go outside!*

His teacher made a chuckling sound. Just as mysteriously as the big hand had appeared, it vanished. Beansie didn't look back. He ran out the door faster than chained lightning.

CHAPTER EIGHT

❖

No Half-pints Allowed

Beansie stumbled outdoors with his dinner bucket. He blinked in the unexpected glare of ground and trees covered with more snow. When did this happen? How many hours, days, weeks had he been trapped indoors? He didn't know. The wind felt fresh on his hot face. Every so often sunlight pierced the gloom.

Free at last! He ditched his dinner bucket beside the schoolhouse where some small children huddled out of the wind. They eagerly gobbled their corn-bread lunches. But Beansie felt too happy to be able to run and jump again to waste time eating.

Some older girls shuffled their feet in the snow and made a huge wheel with spokes and a hub. As soon as they finished, other children pretended to be geese escaping from a fox. They shouted and laughed and dashed down one snow path and up another.

When a new game started and Louisa joined in, she gave Beansie a look that meant, *Don't aggrafret me.* Then she raced up the spokes trampled in the snow as fast as anyone.

Beansie wandered away. On the other side of the clearing, he noticed Skunk Breath and another group dodging from tree to tree, playing tag.

"Tree! Tree!" Skunk Breath shouted. He motioned for Beansie to be on his team.

Beansie copied whatever Skunk Breath did. When Skunk Breath ran, Beansie ran. When Skunk Breath hugged a tree to escape from a chaser, so did Beansie. "Tree! Tree!" called Skunk Breath as he held tight to a sapling.

"Tree! Tree!" Beansie echoed. His face was flushed with happiness. School didn't seem so bad just then.

When the game of tree tag ended, Beansie decided to explore the other side of the schoolhouse. There he discovered four big boys. "Annie

Over!" they called and hurled a fascinating yarn ball over the roof. Then they dashed to the other side of the schoolhouse.

Beansie was curious. He followed them. There he discovered four more boys shoving and chasing the shouting invaders. Amidst the rassling and hollering, a brand-spang-new green scarf flashed past.

"What do you think you're doing here?"

Beansie felt his collar tighten around his throat.

"Travelin' or goin' somewhere?" asked another boy with a front tooth missing. He held his clenched fist in front of Beansie's face. "Go home and tell your ma she wants you."

Beansie blinked hard. He wanted to go home more than anything. But how could he escape when Gruff Voice clutched his coat? "Not doing nothing," Beansie said, almost blubbering. "Leave me go."

"Bet you'd like to try to throw the ball, wouldn't you?"

Beansie nodded, filled with relief.

"Well, you can't." No Tooth laughed.

"What should we do, Sweeny?" Gruff Voice demanded. "Take him down to the crick and stuff him under the ice?"

Beansie trembled. *Oliver Sweeny!* He shut his eyes.

"Let a drove of half-wild hogs full of fight trample him," No Tooth suggested.

"Leave him go."

Beansie opened his eyes and found himself staring at a brand-spang-new green scarf. Oliver Sweeny, the boy who could outrun, outlick, and outholler anybody, cocked his big round head to one side. He tossed the yarn ball back and forth from one hand to the other and inspected Beansie. His eyes were the color of hard hickory nuts. "Looks to me," Oliver said, "like Little-Bean-Boy's obflusticated."

"You lost, Little-Bean-Boy?" Gruff Voice demanded.

Beansie sucked in his trembling lower lip. He didn't know what the right answer might be. He said nothing.

Oliver pocketed the ball. "This part of the school yard," he said, gesturing grandly to the

stumpy open patch, "belongs to us ring-tailed roarers. No half-pints allowed."

Oliver's friends hooted and laughed.

"So take your time but hurry and get out of
here," Oliver said. He ran his hand through his
unruly brown hair that stood in wild spikes on his
head. His arms bulged in his too-small coat. In
one swift, unexpected movement, Oliver shoved
Beansie hard.

Beansie landed in the snow. He lay there
crumpled and shocked but unhurt. Slowly he sat
up and hugged his knees. For a moment he kept
his head down as if that might make Oliver and
the other cackling ring-tailed roarers disappear.
But the boys didn't go away.

"Lose your balance again, Little-Bean-Boy?"
No Tooth demanded.

Beansie struggled to stand. He brushed himself off as best he could. His face burned. He
wanted to punch somebody, but he knew he
couldn't. Oliver and the other boys were too big.
For the first time he understood how humiliated
and angry Louisa must have felt when she landed
in that mud puddle.

"Leave us alone," Oliver said. Then he leaned so close that Beansie could smell the woolly dampness of his brand-spang-new green scarf. "Don't tarry here, Beansie," he whispered. "Ain't safe."

Beansie didn't need to be warned twice. He scurried to the place where he'd left his dinner bucket. None of the other children sitting there paid any attention when he wiped his face with his sleeve. He sat by himself and ate his soggy hoecake. More than anything he longed to go home and sit by the fireplace, where it was warm and safe. Maybe he'd leave right now. Maybe—

Dong-dong-dong!

Too late. It was already time to go back inside.

CHAPTER NINE

❖

Bad-luck Signs

Beansie trudged into school. He didn't notice that the wind had shifted. He didn't see the way the snow suddenly kicked up and blew about. He was too busy thinking about bad-luck signs. Owls flying past the window; breath of a horse on his face; rabbit crossing his path. And now he had to worry about another: the glimpse of a brand-spang-new green scarf. When he saw that sign, he knew he might any moment be stuffed under the ice or locked in the outhouse or trapped inside the woodpile or abandoned under a hog stampede.

School, he decided, was just too dangerous. When he got home he knew what he'd do. He'd tell Pap he wasn't ever going back. He was quitting.

"Come to books!" Master Strike shouted.

"Ain't you got the weary dismals," Skunk Breath said when he saw Beansie climb onto the bench.

Beansie was too homesick to say a word. He was sure if he opened his mouth he'd start to cry. And crying was just one more thing Louisa had forbidden him to do. He studied his scuffed shoe tops and wondered how many hours, how many years would pass before he would be free again.

Soggy coats and hats steamed beside the fireplace and sent up a sour smell. All afternoon the class recited from their readers. But Beansie's feet felt too cold and wet for him to care a thing about a story of a fox and some sour grapes.

Finally Master rang the bell. School ended. How glad Beansie was to escape! He grabbed his dinner bucket and followed the others as they whooped and hollered out of the building into more softly falling snow. It was nearly dark. Beansie raced all the way across the clearing when he remembered he was supposed to walk with Louisa. Where was she?

She trudged toward him with her shawl pulled up on her head. He couldn't see her face very well to tell if the children had bothered her about her freckles. And he didn't really want to talk about what had happened to him at noon recess. "Come on, Beansie," she said. Her voice sounded tired.

Beansie took her hand once no one else could see them. Together they entered the woods, which were filled with shadows. Everything looked different now. The fluffy snow kept falling in bunches. The shapes of covered bushes and rocks reminded Beansie of rabbits and clouds and frogs. He wanted to inspect these, but he couldn't because Louisa kept hurrying him along.

Every so often he caught sight of tracks shuffling ahead of them, following the same trail that Pap had blazed.

"That Oliver Sweeny?" Beansie asked. He pointed with a trembling finger at a trudging shape ahead. He blinked and thought he saw the dreaded brand-spang-new green scarf.

"Sure looks like him," Louisa replied.

What if Oliver's friends were hiding up ahead in the trees, waiting to do something awful? Beansie felt like he might throw up.

"Keep a distance," Louisa said. "Don't get too close."

Beansie nodded. He'd keep his distance all right. He still smarted from Oliver's shove. *Little-Bean-Boy*. The boys' laughter rang in his ears.

Beansie and Louisa followed the path through the brush between the snowy sugar maples. No matter how fast they walked, Oliver seemed to be getting farther and farther ahead. By the time they crossed Crooked Creek, they could not see his brand-spang-new green scarf through the trees.

Something cold fell down Beansie's neck. His legs were tired, but he didn't complain. "Hurry up!" Louisa said.

On and on they walked. Oliver's footprints twisted and turned. They crossed Crooked Creek again. The wind blew snow, so the tracks disappeared completely in some places. "Should we go this way?" Beansie asked. "Or this?"

"I know where we're going," Louisa insisted. She looked up to find Pap's blaze marks. In the snow and darkness they were hard to see.

"Can we rest on this stump?" Beansie asked.

Louisa sat down beside Beansie. She kept fidgeting and looking around as if she was scared. What if she had woods fever? He wasn't sure he could remember the way back by himself. He tried to remember what Pap had said to do: "Keep your eyes peeled for Oliver and follow him."

Oliver had moved too fast and was too far ahead to be of help anymore. The boy who could outrun, outlick, outholler anyone was out of sight. Even his footprints were rapidly vanishing in the drifting snow and wind.

Beansie tried to think. Pap had said he'd stopped being lost when he tried counting his hunting dogs. Beansie didn't have a dog. He chewed on his sleeve and felt miserable.

"Stop doing that," Louisa said. "You'll ruin your coat."

The familiar scolding sound of her voice gave him courage. "Maybe Oliver's lost, too," Beansie said in his most helpful voice.

Louisa put her mittens to her face. She started to cry.

"Don't cry," Beansie said with alarm. "If you don't think you can walk any farther, I'll tote you."

Louisa blew her nose. Beansie took her hand. She stood up. They started walking. On and on they trudged through the snow, which was falling faster and faster. They followed the tracks as they looped between the trees.

Luckily Beansie was close to the ground. Just when Louisa was ready to give up, he found more footprints in the snow. "Oliver went this way!" Beansie said happily.

He and Louisa walked faster. They poked their noses everywhere, like a dog smelling out a trail. On and on they wandered around trees, over hills. Snow blew in their faces and stuck to their eyelashes. They were tired, wet, and hungry, but they kept following the footprints.

"Can't we sit down here and rest?" Louisa asked as if she couldn't walk another step.

"No," Beansie said. "Keep moving."

Soon there would be no light at all. The footprints were filling up with snow. They had to hurry to make out the shapes. What was Oliver thinking? Where was Oliver going? Nothing looked familiar.

Just when Beansie thought he'd never see a house again, they suddenly stumbled into a clearing. Trees vanished. Stumps stood covered with snow. "Over here!" Beansie shouted.

Sure enough, through the darkness and falling snow, they spied the wavering, welcome shape of a candle burning in a window.

CHAPTER TEN

❖

Backward and Forward

Overjoyed, Beansie and his sister hurried toward the cabin. They were so excited, they didn't stop to think who might live there.

"Hello!" Beansie called.

Louisa knocked loudly. "Anyone home?"

The door opened. There stood a woman wrapped in a shawl. She held a candle high. "Who's there?" Her voice had a hard, trembling edge that Beansie did not recognize.

"Louisa and Beansie," Louisa said timidly. "Who are you, ma'am?"

"I'm Missus Sweeny," the woman said. "Been nearly a coon's age since I seen you, child. Come in, both of you, before you catch your death."

It took a moment for Beansie's eyes to adjust to the light from Missus Sweeny's roaring fire. Nervously he looked around the one-room cabin for Oliver. *Where's he hiding?* Neither Beansie nor Louisa had ever been inside Oliver's house before. Even though it was warm and pleasant, Beansie didn't want to linger. He'd rather face a blizzard than meet up with Oliver face-to-face.

"You seen my boy?" Missus Sweeny asked. "He ain't home yet."

Beansie breathed a sigh of relief. Maybe there was still a chance they could escape alive. He glanced at Louisa. She looked nervous, too.

"We followed him for a while, ma'am," Louisa said and gulped. "But after a while all we could find were his footprints in the snow."

Missus Sweeny took their coat and shawl, gave them a hard shake, and motioned for Beansie and Louisa to sit on a bench by the fire. As soon as Beansie sat down, a drowsiness came over him. Missus Sweeny handed both of them a mug of hot sweet cider that tasted different from the kind Ma made but almost as good. "Your parents must be worried sick. I've been waiting for Oliver a long while." She looked as if she might burst into tears any moment. "Where can he be?"

Beansie took a sip of cider and studied Missus Sweeny over the rim of the mug. *Please don't cry. Please don't cry.* "Don't worry," Beansie said. He tried to sound as reassuring as he could. "Oliver knows these woods backward and forward."

Missus Sweeny shook her head. "He's got more luck than sense." She walked to the window and placed the candle on the nearby table. Then she found a big quilt with a design Ma called Four Patch but with different colors and draped it over Beansie and Louisa.

Right away Beansie felt cozy and homesick—all at the same time. He missed Ma. He missed Pap. *What if I never see them again?* Just when he was feeling particularly dismal, an awful stomping and stamping came from outside the cabin door.

Missus Sweeny jumped to her feet. "Maybe that's Oliver."

Louisa tucked her braids inside her collar. Beansie huddled deeper under the blanket. What would Oliver do to them when he found them in his house, sitting by his fire, wrapped in his quilt, drinking his cider?

Missus Sweeny unlatched the door. She held the candle high. Something familiar jangled. "Looks like your family's cow," she said. "You suppose you followed her footprints here?"

Beansie and Louisa hurried to the doorway. "Maybe," said Louisa. She tenderly brushed snow from Bess's head. "You wayward cow. What are you doing?"

"The snow must have confused her, too," said Beansie. "I bet Bess has been wandering the woods backward and forward."

And for the first time that day, Louisa smiled at Beansie. Her grin surprised him.

Bess shook her head. She mooed. She wanted to go home. So did Beansie and Louisa. Missus Sweeny tied a rope to the cow and attached it to the rail fence.

"Don't shut that door!" a voice shouted just when Missus Sweeny was about to come back inside.

Anxiously she peered into the darkness with a candle. "Oliver?" she called.

"I'm coming!" Oliver staggered into view so cloaked with snow that Louisa and Beansie hardly knew him. His face was white. His hair was white. His brand-spang-new green scarf was white. He didn't look one bit like the big, fierce boy who could outrun, outlick, outholler anybody. He was cold and wet and bewildered—just like Beansie and Louisa before they had come inside and sat before the fire.

"Thank goodness you're safe!" Missus Sweeny exclaimed. "Where were you?"

Oliver knocked the snow from his mittens and took off his coat. "Wandered clear off course. That snow was falling so thick, you could hardly spit."

Missus Sweeny took Oliver's coat and handed him another quilt. Oliver sat wrapped up before the fire. So did Beansie and Louisa.

"Pap said," Beansie piped up in his bravest voice, "you knew these woods backward and forward."

Oliver grinned sheepishly. "Guess I don't know as much as everybody thought. Guess I got obflusticated."

"Guess you did," Louisa said and sniffed. "Beansie's the one who helped find our way here. He wasn't obflusticated. Not one bit. Were you, Beansie?"

Beansie blushed. "We followed the cow. We thought it was you."

Oliver chuckled. "You're awful honest for somebody no bigger than a half-pint of cider."

Beansie couldn't help himself. He smiled. He was glad Oliver didn't call him Little-Bean-Boy.

"Snow's stopped," Missus Sweeny said, peering through a crack in the door.

"Maybe I can walk you home," Oliver said to Louisa.

"No, thank you," Louisa replied. Her face turned as bright as a sugar maple. She didn't look one bit like a turkey egg as far as Beansie could tell. "I have my brother for company," she continued. "And Bess can lead us. We're not far from home now."

Hearing those words made Beansie feel important.

Beansie and Louisa thanked Missus Sweeny for letting them share her fire and cider. Oliver

fumbled with Beansie's coat. "Here you go, Beansie," he said. "See you tomorrow at school."

"All right," Beansie said.

Oliver blushed. "Good-bye, Louisa."

"Good-bye," Louisa replied. She hurried out the door.

As they trudged into their own cabin's clearing with Bess, Louisa turned to Beansie and said, "You never gave up trying to find our way even when the snow was so thick you could hardly spit. You're not as puny and no-count as I thought."

"I know," Beansie replied, standing as tall as he could. He reached into his coat pocket. To his complete surprise he discovered a yarn ball. Only Oliver could have put it there. Beansie grinned. *Maybe school won't be so bad after all.*

Just then the cabin doorway filled with light. "Beansie and Louisa," Pap and Ma called, "that you?"

"We're safe!" Beansie shouted. "Bess, too!" Before he knew it, he broke into a run straight for Pap's and Ma's open arms.

GLOSSARY

❖

aggrafret	irritate, aggravate, or make angry or upset
biggety	boastful or full of importance
bumfuzzled	crazy
mulligrubs	discouragement or worry
noggin	mug carved from wood
obflusticated	bewildered or lost
pizzened	poisoned
rassled	wrestled
scawmy	misty
trencher	shallow, wide bowl-like plate carved from wood
whopperjawed	crooked or leaning

AUTHOR'S NOTE

❖

Words and expressions described in this book were commonly used by settlers in Indiana in the nineteenth century. Some of the words' origins may date back to seventeenth century Virginia. *Hoosier Folklore Bulletin* (Volume 5, 1946) and *American Speech* (Volume 14, 1939 and Volumes 16–17, 1941–42) contain early Indiana expressions collected by folklorist Paul G. Brewster and others.

Additional sources include: Logan Esarey's *The Indiana Home* (Crawfordsville, IN: R. E. Banta, 1947); Carl Sandburg's *The American Songbag* (NY: Harcourt Brace, 1927); Writer's Program of the Works Progress Administration in the state of Indiana, *Indiana: A Guide to the Hoosier State* (NY: Oxford University Press, 1941); and Benjamin Botkin's *A Treasury of American Folklore* (NY: Crown, 1944).